bucket

bananas

crayons

balloons

book

birds

picture

shovel

socks

slippers

cake

towel

duck

sand castles

doll

sweater

triangle

flowers

lemonade

chick

boiled egg

sponge

panties

apples

For Carlos

First U.S. edition 1992
First published in Great Britain in 1991 by Walker Books Ltd., London.

ISBN 1-56402-042-8
Library of Congress Catalog Card Number 91-71817
Library of Congress Cataloging-in-Publication information is available.

10 9 8 7 6 5 4 3 2 1

Printed and bound in Hong Kong

Candlewick Press
2067 Massachusetts Avenue
Cambridge, Massachusetts 02140

WORDS AND PICTURES

SIOBHAN DODDS

CANDLEWICK PRESS
CAMBRIDGE, MASSACHUSETTS

Getting Dressed

First I put on my 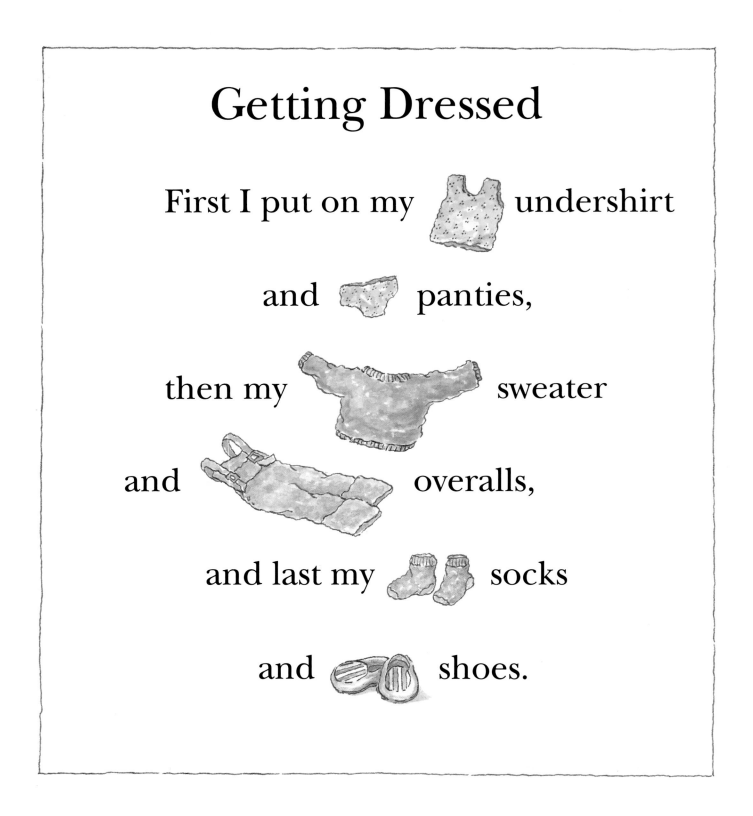 undershirt

and panties,

then my sweater

and overalls,

and last my socks

and shoes.

Breakfast

I have a  bowl of cereal

and a boiled egg.

Daddy always has a cup of coffee.

Mommy likes toast

and jam.

School

We have 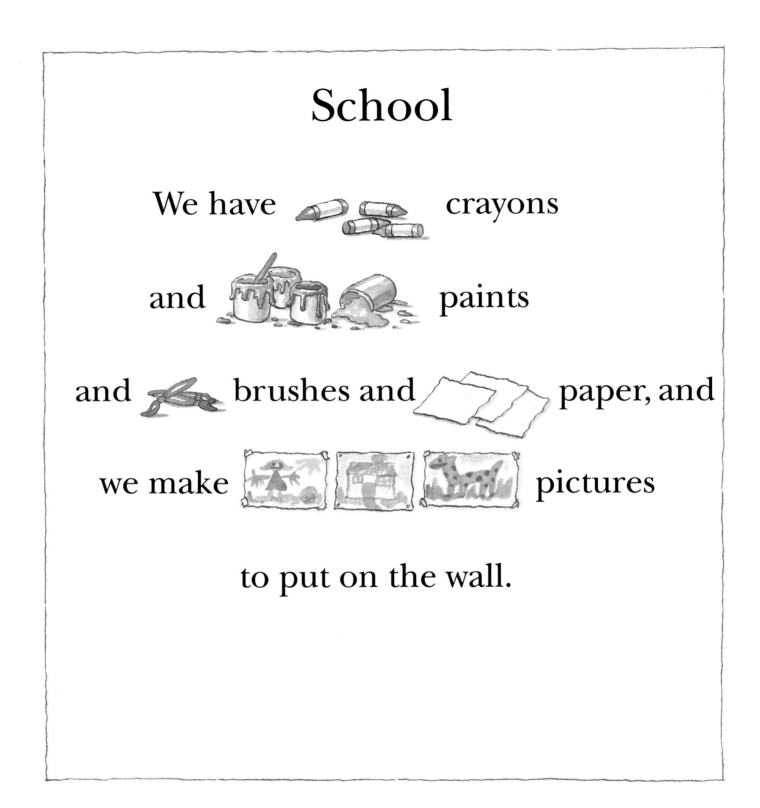 crayons

and paints

and brushes and paper, and

we make pictures

to put on the wall.

Playtime

Jason plays with his  ball,

Mary has her jump rope,

Claire and Lucy put the doll to bed,

and I make a house with blocks.

In the Park

There are lots of  flowers

and birds,

and I like feeding the ducks.

Once my kite

got stuck in a tree.

At the Beach

I like wearing my  sunglasses

and my flip-flops.

I make sand castles

with my bucket

and shovel.

Shopping

Mommy puts the  potatoes,

carrots, and bananas

in her basket.

I carry the peas,

mushrooms, and apples

in mine.

On the Farm

I feed the  hens and

chicks

and help to take care of

the pig, the sheep,

and the calf.

At a Party

We drink  lemonade

and eat cookies and cake.

We all wear party hats

and have balloons

to take home.

Music Time

Our teacher plays the  piano,

Mary is learning the recorder,

I play the triangle,

Jason plays the xylophone,

and Lucy bangs the drum.

Bath Time

I blow  bubbles

and play with my duck.

Mommy washes me with soap

and a sponge

and dries me with a towel.

Bedtime

I take off my  slippers

and get into bed

with Teddy.

Mommy reads me a book.

The clock says 7 o'clock.

Good night!

calf

tree

recorder

jump rope

ball

pig

xylophone

basket

duck

carrots

undershirt

kite

flip-flops

bubbles

toast

sheep

drum

paints

brushes

Teddy

sunglasses

clock

blocks

party hats